A Note From Rick Renner

I am on a personal quest to see a "revival of the Bible" so people can establish their lives on a firm foundation that will stand strong and endure the test as end-time storm winds begin to intensify.

In order to experience a revival of the Bible in your personal life, it is important to take time each day to read, receive, and apply its truths to your life. James tells us that if we will continue in the perfect law of liberty — refusing to be forgetful hearers, but determined to be doers — we will be blessed in our ways. As you watch or listen to the programs in this series and work through this corresponding study guide, I trust you will search the Scriptures and allow the Holy Spirit to help you hear something new from God's Word that applies specifically to your life. I encourage you to be a doer of the Word He reveals to you. Whatever the cost, I assure you — it will be worth it.

> Thy words were found, and I did eat them;
> and thy word was unto me the joy and rejoicing of mine heart:
> for I am called by thy name, O Lord God of hosts.
> — Jeremiah 15:16

Your brother and friend in Jesus Christ,

Rick Renner

Unless otherwise indicated, all scripture quotations are taken from the *King James Version* of the Bible.

Scripture quotations marked (*NLT*) are taken from the *New Living Translation*, copyright © 1996, 2004, 2015 by Tyndale House Foundation. Used by permission of Tyndale House Publishers, Inc., Carol Stream, Illinois 60188. All rights reserved.

How To Get Out of the Trap the Devil Set for You

Copyright © 2019 by Rick Renner
1814 W. Tacoma St.
Broken Arrow, OK 74012-1406

Published by Rick Renner Ministries
www.renner.org

ISBN 13: 978-1-6803-1642-1

eBook ISBN 13: 978-1-6803-1642-1

All rights reserved. No portion of this book may be reproduced or transmitted in any form or by any means — electronic, mechanical, photocopy, recording, scanning, or other — except for brief quotations in critical reviews or articles, without the prior written permission of the Publisher.

How To Use This Study Guide

This five-lesson study guide corresponds to *"How To Get Out of the Trap the Devil Set for You" With Rick Renner* (**Renner TV**). Each lesson in this study guide covers a topic that is addressed during the program series, with questions and references supplied to draw you deeper into your own private study of the Scriptures on this subject.

To derive the most benefit from this study guide, consider the following:

First, watch or listen to the program prior to working through the corresponding lesson in this guide. (Programs can also be viewed at **renner.org** by clicking on the Media/Archives links or on our Renner Ministries YouTube channel.)

Second, take the time to look up the scriptures included in each lesson. Prayerfully consider their application to your own life.

Third, use a journal or notebook to make note of your answers to each lesson's Study Questions and Practical Application challenges.

Fourth, invest specific time in prayer and in the Word of God to consult with the Holy Spirit. Write down the scriptures or insights He reveals to you.

Finally, take action! Whatever the Lord tells you to do according to His Word, do it.

For added insights on this subject, it is recommended that you obtain Rick Renner's book *Life in the Combat Zone*. You may also select from Rick's other available resources by placing your order at **renner.org** or by calling 1-800-742-5593.

LESSON 1

TOPIC
The Brother of Jesus

SCRIPTURES
1. **James 1:1** — James, a servant of God and of the Lord Jesus Christ, to the twelve tribes which are scattered abroad, greeting.
2. **Matthew 13:55, 56** — Is not this the carpenter's son? Is not his mother called Mary? And his brethren, James, and Joses, and Simon, and Judas? And his sisters, are they not all with us? Whence then hath this man all these things?
3. **Acts 16:31** — And they said, Believe on the Lord Jesus Christ, and thou shalt be saved, and thy house.

GREEK WORDS
1. "servant" — δοῦλος (*doulos*): slave; one who is completely swallowed up in the will of another
2. "scattered abroad" — διασπορά (*diaspora*): the random scattering of seed; used to depict the scattering of Jewish believers

SYNOPSIS
The five lessons in this study on ***How To Get Out of the Trap the Devil Set for You*** will focus on the following topics:

- The Brother of Jesus
- What God Does and Never Does
- The Attitude You Need To Get Out of Your Mess
- If You Need Wisdom
- The Right Way To Ask in Faith

The emphasis of this lesson:

James, who wrote the book of James, was Jesus' half-brother and proof that God specializes in calling families to work together to fulfill His will.

Located in southern Turkey on the Syrian border is an ancient landmark called the Titus Tunnel. At first glance, it looks like a cave, but it isn't. It is a manmade channel that was chiseled out of rock during the First Century, created to redirect floodwaters away from the Port of Salacia.

Roman Emperor Vespasian began the project, giving the order for servants, slaves, criminals, and even some Roman soldiers to perform the excavation. His son Titus continued the venture during his reign. After attacking the city of Jerusalem, he forced many captured Jews to carry on the work. Emperor Domitian, Vespasian's brother and a ruthless Christian-killer, took on the task after Titus, enslaving many believers whose lives he viewed as worthless.

As prisoners, these Christians were given only bread and water to live on, which was not enough for subsistence in such a place. Thus, many of them died. As believers were forced to labor on the construction of this tunnel, they must have wondered, *God, is this what You planned for our lives? We believe the Gospel, yet we have ended up enslaved in this place. Are You allowing this to happen? Is there any way out of this mess we're in?*

These were the same questions believers in the First Century were asking the apostle James after being persecuted and scattered abroad across the Roman Empire because of their faith. In response, James wrote the book bearing his name, effectively addressing their doubts and concerns.

Maybe *you're* trapped in a challenging situation and are asking the same kinds of questions. These lessons will provide solid answers and truth in which you can rest and *trust*.

James and the Family of Jesus

James was the half-brother of Jesus. He and Jesus had the same mother, but they didn't have the same father. Jesus' Father was God, and James' father was Joseph. We know that Mary was "highly favored and blessed among women" (*see* Luke 1:28); Joseph was very special too. He was a spiritual man open to the voice of the Holy Spirit through dreams, visions, and angelic visitations. He was willing and obedient to do whatever God directed him to do. Therefore, he was purposely selected by God to be Jesus' natural father.

As you study Scripture, you will find that Jesus had several siblings: four brothers and at least two sisters. Matthew 1:25 clearly states that Mary and

Joseph had no sexual relationship until after the birth of Jesus. Therefore, Christ was conceived supernaturally and was born as the Son of God. After His birth, Mary and Joseph had a normal marital relationship, bringing forth several other children. Their names are listed in Matthew 13:55.

Obviously, their firstborn Son was Jesus, who was and is God in the flesh. James, who wrote the book bearing his name, was next, followed by his brother Joseph, who was obviously named after their father. Simon was the third son in the family, and Jude, who wrote the book of Jude, was the fourth. Thus, Jesus had four brothers, and according to Matthew 13:56, He also had "sisters." In Greek, this word is plural, which means there were at least two, but possibly more.

This was a remarkable family indeed. It's interesting to note that Mary, the mother of Jesus, as well as His four brothers and sisters were all present in the Upper Room on the Day of Pentecost (*see* Acts 1:13, 14), which means they were all filled with the Holy Spirit and spoke in tongues. Eventually, each member of Jesus' family became involved in ministry, but that was not the way they started out.

Opposition From Within

In John 7:5, the Bible explicitly tells us that Jesus' brothers did not believe in Him during the course of His life. In fact, we know from early Christian writings that James was quite an adversary of Jesus. Some may ask, "How could one grow up in the same household with Jesus and be His personal adversary?" Well, try to imagine what it would be like growing up in a family where your elder brother was God in the flesh. Jesus never did anything wrong and was always commended for doing everything right!

More than likely, James and his younger siblings were often compared to Jesus, perhaps regularly hearing the words, "Why can't you be more like Jesus?" Apparently, James became so fed up with living in the shadow of perfection that he developed a real resentment toward Jesus and didn't like Him at all. Some early writers even say that James was an "opponent of Jesus' ministry."

Jesus was aware of the tension and turmoil within James. It was so important to resolve it that one of the first things Jesus did after being raised from the dead was to appear to him. When James saw Jesus resurrected from the dead, he finally understood why his brother was so good. He came to realize his brother was more than just his brother — his brother was the Messiah, God in the flesh.

At that moment, James was radically converted and became not only a believer, but also the leader of the Church in Jerusalem. His leadership role became so pivotal that we read about it in Acts chapter 15. When the apostle Paul came to Jerusalem to explain to the leadership how the Gentiles were coming to Christ, it was James who mediated that conference (*see* Galatians 1:19). He was the leading voice in the city of Jerusalem at that time, and you can imagine his level of notoriety simply because he was the natural brother of Jesus.

God Specializes in Calling Entire Families

Mary and Joseph were remarkable parents who raised an entire family that served in ministry. Jesus, their firstborn, was the Messiah. James became the head of the Church in Jerusalem and wrote the book of James. Jude was very active and wrote Jude, the second to last book of the New Testament. And early Christian writers tell us Jesus' sisters were also involved in ministry.

God is in the business of calling and equipping entire families to serve in His Kingdom. We see this pattern again and again in Scripture. Looking at the book of Genesis, we see that God called Noah and his wife and three sons and their wives to replenish the earth after the flood. He called Abraham and Sarah and their entire lineage. This included Isaac and Rebekah, as well as Jacob and his 12 sons. Then there was Moses and his brother Aaron and their sister Miriam, who were all called into ministry.

When we come to the New Testament, the family pattern continues. We've seen Mary and Joseph and their children. We also have Zachariah, Elizabeth, and their son John the Baptist as an example along with two sets of brothers — James and John "the sons of Zebedee" and Peter and Andrew.

Interestingly, the apostle Paul had two family members who got saved before he did. Romans 16:7 identifies them as "Andronicus and Junia," his kinsmen. Scripture says they were both apostles. Thus, there were three apostles in the same family.

Another family God called into ministry is that of Barnabas, the "son of encouragement." His sister's name was Mary, and she was well-known among the early Church. She lived in the city of Jerusalem and had a very large apartment with a big room. It was in that extra-large room that the Day of Pentecost took place and the 120 who were gathered were all baptized in the Holy Spirit.

Mary, Barnabas' sister, also had a son who got saved and became involved in ministry. His name was John Mark — the same John Mark who served as a travel companion of Paul and Barnabas and later became a scribe for the apostle Peter. At that time, he lived in Rome and began to write down the Gospel as Peter dictated it. This account became known as the gospel of Mark. It is called by this name because John Mark wrote it, but it is actually the Gospel according to Peter.

It All Starts With One Individual

When God saves entire families, you will find that His call was initiated with one person having an encounter with Him. Noah was the one in his family who developed the habit of walking with God, and it affected his whole family. Likewise, Abraham is the one in his family who first heard and responded to God's invitation to follow Him — and his wife, Sarah, and their son Isaac pursued after him. The same can be said of Jacob and his family, Moses and his family, and all the families who followed Christ in the New Testament.

There is a powerful promise in Acts 16:31, which says, "…Believe on the Lord Jesus Christ, and thou shalt be saved, and thy house." Although this doesn't mean that everyone in your family will instantly be born again just because you get saved, it promises that if you will believe on the Lord Jesus Christ and surrender your life to Him, your encounter with Him will be so dramatic and impactful that eventually it will bring your whole family to Christ.

Make no mistake: God desires to save your entire family. He doesn't want anyone to die without knowing Him. Eternal punishment in hell was reserved for the devil and his angels; God wants everyone to be saved (*see* 1 Timothy 2:4). He has a special, one-of-a-kind assignment for you and each member of your family to accomplish. The witness of your life and the prayers of your lips build a bridge for them to cross into the Kingdom.

The End of James' Life

Early Christian writers tell us that James was the most visible believer in the city of Jerusalem toward the end of his life. That being the case, the

Jewish religious leaders tried to cut a deal with him. Basically, they came to him and said, "James, we know that Jesus was a fraud, and we think you share in this belief. We would like to make a deal with you, and if you agree to work with us, we will promote you in every way we can."

Interestingly, the Jewish leaders lured James to the pinnacle of the temple — the same place the devil took Jesus when he tempted Him while in the desert. This lets us know that the enemy is not very creative. He just keeps doing the same things over and over.

Once James reached the pinnacle of the temple, the religious leaders told him to publicly renounce Jesus. They had blown their shofars and gathered people from all across Jerusalem to hear James, the half-brother of Jesus, denounce Christ. By that time, a crowd had formed around the base of the temple, waiting to hear what this leader of the Christian Church had to say.

"This Jesus," James declared, in effect, "whom you have slain with wicked hands, God raised back to life! He is no longer dead but alive and seated at the Father's right hand. In the future, He is going to come in the clouds of glory to judge the living and the dead."

The religious leaders were infuriated by James' declaration. Instead of renouncing Jesus as they wanted, he exalted Him and made it appear that they were in agreement with his statement. In a blind rage, they collectively pushed James off the edge of the pinnacle of the temple, and he plummeted to the ground. They then came with clubs and beat him to death. The man who was once an opponent of Jesus became a committed Christian and died in faith.

James, a Servant of the Lord Jesus Christ

In James 1:1, James described himself as "a servant of God and of the Lord Jesus Christ, to the twelve tribes which are scattered abroad, greeting." The word "servant" here is the Greek word *doulos*. It is used throughout the New Testament to describe every believer. It depicts *a slave; one who is completely swallowed up in the will of another*. By using the word *doulos*, James was saying, "I'm a sold-out servant of God — lock, stock, and barrel. I've surrendered everything I have, and I live for only one purpose — to do the will of God and the Lord Jesus Christ."

It's interesting to note that the word "and" in verse 1 is the Greek word *kai*, which can be translated as we see it in the *King James Version*, or it can also be used as a qualifying statement. In this verse, *kai* could be translated, "James, the servant of God, *who is* of the Lord Jesus Christ."

Another word to note in this verse is "Lord" — the Greek word *Kurios*. In the Septuagint, which is the Greek version of the Old Testament that James would have been reading, the word "Lord" (*Kurios*) is translated *Jehovah*. Moreover, the word "Christ" is the Greek word *Christos*, which is the New Testament word for *Messiah*.

This means that when James called Jesus, "The Lord Jesus Christ," he was declaring that Jesus was Jehovah in the flesh. Likewise, every time you say, "The Lord Jesus Christ," you are declaring that Jesus is Jehovah God in the flesh, the Messiah. He was not just a prophet or a good man that lived. He is the Lord Jesus Christ. And James said he was a servant of Him. We are called to be servants of Him as well.

STUDY QUESTIONS

Study to shew thyself approved unto God, a workman that needeth not to be ashamed, rightly dividing the word of truth.
— 2 Timothy 2:15

1. What new insights did you learn about Jesus' family? About the apostle James? What about how God calls entire families?
2. It is God's will to save your entire family. Take a few minutes to meditate on these verses: Acts 16:31; First Timothy 2:1-4; Titus 2:11; and Second Peter 3:9. What is the Holy Spirit showing you in these passages about His desire to bring salvation and about your part in helping bring it to pass?

PRACTICAL APPLICATION

But be ye doers of the word, and not hearers only, deceiving your own selves.
— James 1:22

1. The definition of the word "servant" (*doulos*) is *one who is completely swallowed up in the will of another*. Would you say this describes your relationship with Jesus? If so, what evidence in your life confirms this?

LESSON 2

TOPIC
What God Does and Never Does

SCRIPTURES
1. **Acts 16:31** — And they said, Believe on the Lord Jesus Christ, and thou shalt be saved, and thy house.
2. **James 1:1** — James, a servant of God and of the Lord Jesus Christ, to the twelve tribes which are scattered abroad, greeting.
3. **James 1:13** — Let no man say when he is tempted, I am tempted of God: for God cannot be tempted with evil, neither tempteth he any man
4. **Acts 8:1** — And Saul was consenting unto his death. And at that time there was a great persecution against the church which was at Jerusalem; and they were all scattered abroad throughout the regions of Judaea and Samaria, except the apostles.

GREEK WORDS
1. "servant" — **δοῦλος** (*doulos*): slave; one who is completely swallowed up in the will of another
2. "scattered abroad" — **διασπορά** (*diaspora*): the random scattering of seed; used to depict the scattering of Jewish believers
3. "great" — **μέγας** (*megas*): big, great, huge, or enormous
4. "persecution" — **διώκω** (*dioko*): to pursue; pictured the actions of a hunter who followed after an animal to apprehend, capture, and kill it
5. "tempted" — **πειράζω** (*peiradzo*): to test, try, or tempt; to cause one to fail, to falter, to stumble, or to bring destruction; depicts a calculated test to bring about failure; used to denote the actions of the devil, the tempter, or of the Pharisees and Sadducees
6. "of" — **ἀπό** (*apo*): away from; denotes something done from a distance or something that is done remotely
7. "evil" — **κακός** (*kakos*): evil, vile, foul, or destructive

SYNOPSIS

The Titus Tunnel, or Vespasianus Titus Tunnel, is located near the ancient Port of Salacia in what is today southern Turkey. It is nearly 100 meters long (4,600 feet), and it took more than 100 years to complete. There is nothing about this passageway that is natural. In fact, if you were to look closely at its walls today, you can still see the marks left behind by the hammers and chisels used to carve through solid rock.

The Port of Salacia was being flooded with excessive rain water that was washing down from the mountains. To overcome this problem, Roman Emperor Vespasian ordered that a channel be created. The manpower harnessed to perform this task was made up primarily of prisoners and soldiers.

Vespasian began the project, and it was continued by his son Titus. The bulk of the work, however, was overseen by Domitian, Vespasian's brother. Domitian was a ruthless Christian-killer who enslaved many believers to carry out the job, feeding them only bread and water. It is estimated that tens of thousands of Christians died while working on the Titus Tunnel.

Knowing the extreme hardship these believers endured, it is likely that they struggled mentally and emotionally and cried out to God, asking Him, "Is this what You planned for my life, Lord? Are You allowing this to take place for some unknown reason? If so, why? Have I done something wrong to be trapped and treated like this? Is there any way out of this place?"

The apostle James had to deal with questions just like these as he was leading the church in Jerusalem in those early days. Many believers were being persecuted for their faith in Christ, and James was tasked with the job of helping them know and understand *what God does* and *what He never does*.

The emphasis of this lesson:

When it comes to trials and troubles, there are certain things God will always do and other things He will never do. In order for you to escape the trap the devil has set for you, it is vital for you to understand and think correctly concerning God and His will.

From Our Last Lesson

James was the half-brother of Jesus. The two of them had the same mother but different fathers. Jesus' Father was God, and James' father was Joseph. We also discovered that Jesus had at least two sisters and four brothers — James, Joseph, Simon, and Jude (*see* Matthew 13:55, 56). James wrote the book of James and became the bishop of the church of Jerusalem. When Jesus' brother Jude wrote the book of Jude, he identified himself as "…the servant of Jesus Christ, and brother of James…" (Jude 1).

Mary and Joseph had raised an amazing family, all of which served in some aspect of ministry. This gives us a picture of God's desire to save entire families — including yours. Although your family may not be called to full-time ministry, God has a plan for every member of your family and wants to place His mark on each one. And He promises in Acts 16:31 that if you "…believe on the Lord Jesus Christ, and thou shalt be saved, and thy house."

Does this mean everyone in your family is automatically going to get saved as a result of your salvation? No. It means that when you get saved, you can claim this promise, and salvation will eventually come to your whole family.

Believers Had Been 'Scattered Abroad'

James 1:1 tells us clearly who James was writing to. It says, "James, a servant of God and of the Lord Jesus Christ, to the twelve tribes which are scattered abroad, greeting." The phrase "scattered abroad" is very important. It is the Greek word *diaspora*, and it describes *the random scattering of seed*. Here it is used to depict the scattering of Jewish believers.

In the world of the New Testament, there were two ways of planting seed. The first way was to methodically plant one seed after another in a nice, neat, orderly row. The second way was to carry a whole satchel of seed and to randomly toss the seed all around. This is a picture of what "scattered abroad" (*diaspora*) means.

By understanding this word, we understand what happened to the recipients of James' letter. These precious believers had been ripped out of their homelands, their jobs, and their homes. Many had been separated from their families. Like seed being sown, they had been randomly scattered all over the eastern lands of the Roman Empire.

Clearly, the enemy was behind the scattering of the Church. He thought dispersing believers would stomp out the fire of the Spirit and stop the Church from spreading. However, the exact opposite took place. His efforts of scattering believers served to seed the Gospel into many lands throughout the known world. Although God didn't orchestrate the dispersion, He certainly used it to advance His Kingdom and bring salvation to people far and wide. It is the same thing He will do with the enemy's attacks in your life — He will work them together for your good (*see* Romans 8:28).

When the Scattering Began

By the time of Acts chapter 8, the Church was about five years old and just beginning to experience severe persecution. Stephen had just been stoned (*see* Acts 7:54-60), and Acts 8:1 says, "Saul was consenting unto his death. And at that time there was a great persecution against the church which was at Jerusalem; and they were all scattered abroad throughout the regions of Judaea and Samaria, except the apostles."

There are a few words to notice in this verse, starting with the word "great." It is from the Greek word *megas*, which means *big, great, huge,* or *enormous*. Next is the word "persecution," which is a derivative of the Greek word *dioko*, which means *to pursue*. This is *a hunting term that pictured the actions of a hunter who aggressively followed after an animal to apprehend, capture, and kill it.* That is what the word "persecution" means.

Putting the meanings of *megas* and *dioko* together, this verse could be translated, "About that time, there unexpectedly arose a massive hunt against the Church in Jerusalem." The Jewish leaders, led by Saul (who later became the apostle Paul), began to search for believers. Like hunters, they camouflaged themselves and wormed their way into believers' meetings in order to identify and destroy them.

Acts 8:3 tells us they were going house-to-house in Jerusalem to arrest and imprison Christians. It was at that time that believers were "scattered abroad" throughout Judea and Samaria. Interestingly, the same Greek word *diaspora*, translated as "scattered abroad," is used in both Acts chapter 8 and James chapter 1.

Some scholars have said that James was writing to *all* Jews who lived throughout the Roman Empire, but that is technically incorrect. He was writing to Christians who had come to Christ and had been ripped from their homes and families and had lost their jobs or businesses as a result of their faith in Jesus. These were believers who had been terribly mistreated, some of them beaten, and scattered abroad. They were very disconnected, discouraged, and suffering emotional and mental pain. They were left with many questions — including one question that many suffering believers ask today: "Did God cause or allow this terrible thing to happen in my life?"

A Dissection of James 1:13

James responded to this question in James 1:13. He said, "Let no man say when he is tempted, I am tempted of God: for God cannot be tempted with evil, neither tempteth he any man." However, the way this reads in the Greek is quite different than in the *King James Version*.

First, the verse opens with the phrase "Let no man say." In Greek, this is a very strong rebuke or prohibition that literally means, "I hear what you are saying, and I don't like it; I won't tolerate it any longer. Stop saying what you're saying, and never say it again."

What were these believers saying? They were saying when they were tempted that they were "tempted of God."

The word "tempted" here is a translation of the Greek word *peiradzo*, which means *to test, try, or* tempt; *to cause one to fail, to falter, to stumble,* or *to bring destruction into a person's life*. It depicts *a calculated test to bring about failure*.

It's interesting to note that when we see the word *peiradzo* used throughout the New Testament, it often describes the actions of the devil, the tempter, when he *tries* or *tests* people. This describes Satan's consistent attempts to bring people down and destroy them. That is what Satan attempted to do to Jesus when He was in the wilderness fasting for 40 days. Satan administered a calculated series of temptations when Jesus was weak in order to derail Him from the Father's will. But it didn't work.

The word *peiradzo* is also used in the in the New Testament to describe the behavior of the Pharisees and Sadducees when they tested Jesus. With their clever words they tried to trap Him and bring Him down. They were very calculated, and their efforts were all aimed at causing Jesus to stumble, fall, and be destroyed.

Also notice the word "of" in verse 13. Although it may seem ordinary and insignificant, it may be the most important word of all. "Of" is the

Greek word *apo*, which means *away from*. It denotes *something done from a distance* or *something that is done remotely*. Essentially, when the believers wrote to James concerning the suffering they were experiencing, they said, "We realize that God has not personally caused the pain of these situations. But as God, He is still sovereign and in control of everything. If He had wanted to stop these tragic events, He could have. Therefore, since these terrible things have not been stopped, we calculate that God — from a distance (remotely and indirectly) — has somehow allowed these events to come into our lives."

To this line of thinking, James reacted strongly. He told believers, "Stop it! Don't ever say that again. How dare you say that your lives are being crushed, decimated, and destroyed by the remote, permissive will of God." Again, this is the meaning of the phrase, "Let no man say."

James then continued by saying, "…For God cannot be tempted with evil, neither tempteth he any man." The phrase "cannot be tempted" is the Greek word *apeirasmos*. The word *peirasmos* means *a test or a trial*. When the letter *"a"* is placed in front of it, it means *God is unable to be tested and tried by evil*.

The word "evil" is the Greek word *kakos*, which describes *something evil, vile, foul*, or *destructive*. Clearly, God has no personal experience with "evil." When "evil" tried to come into Heaven in the person of Lucifer, God put a stop to it by casting Satan and those who rebelled with him out of His presence. There is no evil in Heaven, and God doesn't bring evil into your life to test you. It is something He simply cannot do.

If you think God permits evil to come into your life, you will remain in the evil trap of the enemy. However, if you think correctly and understand that the situation you're facing is not sent from God, you will fight against it. Right thinking about trouble and trials is the first step to getting out of your trap.

STUDY QUESTIONS

Study to shew thyself approved unto God, a workman that needeth not to be ashamed, rightly dividing the word of truth.
— 2 Timothy 2:15

1. What have these first two lessons taught you about the Titus Tunnel located in southern Turkey? How does this real-life illustration help you understand and put into perspective the difficult situations you face in life?
2. It is very important to know the true origin of temptation. Look up these scriptures and identify where temptation comes from, as well as any specific actions you need to take to guard or fight against it.
   - Genesis 3:1; Second Corinthians 11:3; James 4:7, 8; First Peter 5:8-11
   - First Timothy 6:6-11
   - James 4:1-3; Second Peter 2:18
3. Take a few moments to meditate on First Corinthians 10:13 and Hebrews 2:17 and 18. Then in your own words, describe what God has promised you when you're faced with temptation.

PRACTICAL APPLICATION

But be ye doers of the word, and not hearers only, deceiving your own selves.
—James 1:22

1. Have you ever asked, "Where is all this trouble coming from?" Or have you wondered, *Is God testing me by allowing this evil situation in my life?* If so, briefly describe the situation.
2. How are you seeing *God* differently after going through this lesson?
3. How do you see your *situation* differently?
4. What action steps do you sense you need to take at this point?

LESSON 3

TOPIC
The Attitude You Need To Get You Out of Your Mess

SCRIPTURES

1. **James 1:1, 2** — James, a servant of God and of the Lord Jesus Christ, to the twelve tribes which are scattered abroad, greeting. My brethren, count it all joy when ye fall into divers temptations.

2. **Acts 8:1** — And Saul was consenting unto his death. And at that time there was a great persecution against the church which was at Jerusalem; and they were all scattered abroad throughout the regions of Judaea and Samaria, except the apostles.

3. **James 1:13** — Let no man say when he is tempted, I am tempted of God: for God cannot be tempted with evil, neither tempteth he any man

4. **James 1:17** — Every good gift and every perfect gift is from above, and cometh down from the Father of lights, with whom is no variableness, neither shadow of turning.

GREEK WORDS

1. "scattered abroad" — διασπορά (*diaspora*): the random scattering of seed; used to depict the scattering of Jewish believers

2. "great" — μέγας (*megas*): big, great, huge, or enormous

3. "persecution" — διώκω (*dioko*): pursue; pictured the actions of a hunter who followed after an animal to apprehend, capture, and kill it

4. "tempted" — πειράζω (*peiradzo*): to test, try, or tempt; to cause one to fail, to falter, to stumble, or to bring destruction; depicts a calculated test to bring about failure; used to denote the actions of the devil, the tempter, or of the Pharisees and Sadducees

5. "of" — ἀπὸ (*apo*): away from; denotes something done from a distance or something that is done remotely

6. "evil" — κακός (*kakos*): evil, vile, foul, or destructive

7. "good" — ἀγαθός (*agathos*): anything good, beneficial, or profitable

8. "gift" — δόσις (*dosis*): perpetual giving from God; the habitual giving of God
9. "perfect" — τέλειον (*teleion*): mature, complete, or perfect
10. "cometh down" — καταβαίνω (*katabaino*): to be dominated or subjugated by something coming down very hard, like a downpour of rain

SYNOPSIS

As noted in previous lessons, the Titus Tunnel is quite a remarkable structure. It is approximately 4,600 feet long, 18 feet wide, and 21 feet high. It was carved out of rock with hammers and chisels primarily by Jews, but also by Christians who were captured and forced into labor. The project began under Emperor Vespasian, continued under his son Titus, and was then overseen by Emperor Domitian, Vespasian's brother. It is called the Titus Tunnel because the lion's share of construction was done during Titus' reign.

It is estimated that 10,000 Christians at a time were working to open this passageway. They barely existed on a diet of bread and water, and some died of malnutrition or disease. In the 100 years that it took to complete this monumental project, many believers undoubtedly felt abandoned by God and questioned within themselves, *Is this what You planned for my life, Lord? Will I ever get out of this place of entrapment?* In your own circumstances, you may have wondered the same thing yourself. The good news is that there is a way out, and having the right attitude is a major key to your escape.

The emphasis of this lesson:

In the midst of suffering, it's vital to have the right view of God. Believing He is the source of suffering, or that He allows it for some reason, will only keep you trapped. Knowing there is no trace of evil in Him and that He only gives what is good is a major key to escaping any trap the devil has set for you.

A Time of Great Persecution and Scattering

As we have learned, James was the head of the Church of Jerusalem, and many believers reached out to him with questions about the suffering they were experiencing. These Christians had been "scattered abroad" across the eastern part of the Roman Empire. "Scattered abroad" is the Greek word *diaspora*, and it describes *one of the processes for planting seed.*

In the First Century world, seed was either planted in a nice, neat row, one seed at a time, or it was planted randomly. The word *diaspora* describes *the random scattering of seed.* The sower would reach his hand into a satchel of seed, grab a handful, and then randomly scatter it over a field, throwing a little here and a little there. This is a picture of what happened to believers. Like seed seized by the hand of the sower, they were taken away from family and friends, removed from their homes and jobs, and randomly scattered to other places. They suffered great persecution for their faith in Christ.

The death of Stephen at the hands of the religious leaders marked the beginning of this dispersion and increased persecution against the Church. This was about five years after the day of Pentecost. Acts 8:1 says, "And Saul was consenting unto his [Stephen's] death. And at that time there was a great persecution against the church which was at Jerusalem; and they were all scattered abroad throughout the regions of Judaea and Samaria, except the apostles."

We saw in the last lesson that the words "great persecution" basically mean *a massive hunt.* Led by Saul, who later became the apostle Paul, a house-to-house hunt was launched throughout Jerusalem. Like animals aggressively tracked by hunters, Christians ran for their lives to escape the murderous clutches of Saul and the religious leaders. One went here, another was scattered there, and so on. It was to these suffering believers that the apostle James addressed his letter.

Have the Right View of God

One main idea of James' letter was that of temptation. The first thing James told the *diaspora* was to "…count it all joy when ye fall into divers temptations" (James 1:2). He also told them, "Let no man say when he is tempted, I am tempted of God: for God cannot be tempted with evil, neither tempteth he any man" (v. 13).

"Let no man say" is a very strong rebuke or prohibition in the original Greek; James was forbidding them to say what they had been saying. "Let no man say" could be translated, "I hear what you're saying, and I don't agree with it. So stop it and stop it now. I don't want to hear it anymore."

This was a reaction to believers who were saying, "God is tempting me," which was not true.

"Tempted" is the Greek word *peiradzo*, which means *to test, try, or tempt; to cause one to fail, to falter, to stumble, or to bring destruction*. It depicts *a calculated test to bring about failure*. It is used throughout the New Testament to denote *the actions of the devil, the tempter, or of the Pharisees and Sadducees*. For example, the devil brought a calculated test against Jesus in the wilderness to take Him down. He also worked through the Jewish leaders, bringing questions, arguments, and accusations against Jesus to try to entrap Him and ruin His reputation.

The word *peiradzo* connotes a premeditated attack. There is nothing accidental about it. It carries the idea of being crushed, devastated, and destroyed. This describes what many believers in the First Century were experiencing.

"Of God" is also an important phrase to understand. The word "of" in Greek can be translated from one of two words. One of the words for "of" is *hupo*, and it implies *direct agency*. In other words, if *hupo* had been used in this verse, it would have meant the believers were saying, "God Himself is doing this destructive things to us." However, the word *hupo* was not used here.

Instead, the word for "of" used here is the Greek word *apo*, and it means *to do something from a distance or remotely*. By using the word *apo*, believers were indirectly accusing God for the hardships they were experiencing. It was as if they were saying, "God is not personally bringing these troubles against us, but He is sovereign in all things. If He had wanted to stop it, He could have stopped it, but He didn't. Therefore — *apo* — from a distance, He is allowing these tragic events to come into our lives for some strange reason."

This is a religious way of thinking, and while it might sound sanctimonious, it is wrong. It was to this that James said, "Stop talking like this — stop it now. *Let no man say* when he is being tempted (crushed, devastated, and destroyed) that God is allowing it for some mysterious reason."

"For God cannot be tempted with evil, neither tempteth he any man." That is the next part of James 1:13. The phrase "God cannot be tempted" is the Greek word *apeirasmos*. The word *peirasmos* means *to be tried* or *to be tempted*. When the letter "a" is placed at the front of *peirasmos* to form *apeirasmos*, it signifies that *God cannot be tempted with evil*. He is totally absent of that quality. Nothing in Him responds to evil, and He has no experience with evil.

When "evil" — the Greek word *kakos*, describing *something evil, vile, foul, or destructive* — tried to enter Heaven through Lucifer's wrong choices, God kicked him and his rebellious cohorts out of His presence. There is nothing evil, vile, or foul in God — therefore, He cannot do anything evil, vile, or foul to anyone. This is such a crucial principle that James said about it, "Do not err, my beloved brethren" (James 1:16). In other words, he was saying, "On this point, do not make a mistake."

Think about it. If you believe that God has allowed cancer into your life, then you will embrace it. You certainly wouldn't fight it. And if you did, you couldn't do it wholeheartedly. If you think God allowed divorce, a car accident, or some other tragedy in your life, rather than resist it, you will try to embrace it with grace so God can "do His work in you."

But God doesn't work that way. He doesn't have any evil in Him with which to tempt or test you. This is precisely why James said, "For God cannot be tempted with evil, neither tempteth he any man" (James 1:13).

God Only Gives Us What Is Good

So if God doesn't give — bring or allow — evil, what *does* He give? James 1:17 answers this question perfectly: "Every good gift and every perfect gift is from above, and cometh down from the Father of lights, with whom is no variableness, neither shadow of turning."

Notice the word "good" here. It is the Greek word *agathos*, which describes *anything good, beneficial,* or *profitable*. When God sends something your way, it will always be good and bring a positive benefit to your life.

How often does God bring good, beneficial things into your life? That is a good question, and the answer is found in the meaning of the word "gift."

The Greek word for "gift" is *dosis*, and it describes *perpetual giving from God*. In other words, this is not a single gift; it is describing *the habitual giving of God*. In fact, the phrase "every good gift" could be translated, "*Every good habitual giving.*"

Good Gift — Perfect Gift

To make sure we really understand this, the Holy Spirit added to "every good gift" the phrase "and every perfect gift." The word "perfect" in Greek is the word *teleion*, and it describes *something mature, complete,* or *perfect.* This means we could translate the verse, *"Every good habitual giving of God is completing, maturing, and perfecting."* What comes from God *adds to you;* it doesn't *take away.*

So one would only need to ask the questions: Does cancer add to your life or take away? What about other forms of sickness or disease, such as arthritis, Parkinson's disease, leukemia, migraines, infertility, etc.? Do they add to your life or take away? What about house fires, floods, and other disasters? What about poverty and lack? Are these beneficial and completing? *No.*

Sickness, disasters, and poverty don't add to life; they take away from it. Therefore, none of these is from God. Only "good and perfect gifts" come from above. Every deadly, damaging, and destructive thing is from below.

His Gifts Come Like a Downpour

James makes it clear that "every good gift and every perfect gift is from above, and cometh down from the Father of lights…" (James 1:17). The phrase "cometh down" is the Greek word *katabaino*. It is the compound of two words: the word *kata*, which describes *something that comes down so hard it is dominating or subjugating;* and the word *baino*, which means *to step down.* It is the same word one would use to describe walking down a flight of stairs. When the words *kata* and *baino* are compounded to form *katabaino*, it means *to be dominated or subjugated by something coming down very hard, like a downpour of rain.*

Have you ever been driving in a downpour, and the rain was coming down so hard and heavy that you couldn't see anything in front of you? The downpour was so dominating that you had to pull over to the side of the road and wait for the rain to stop? That describes the meaning of the phrase "cometh down" and indicates how God is sending His good and perfect gifts to you.

Someone may say, "If God is pouring good and perfect gifts on me, why am I not hit by one of those downpours at least occasionally?" The answer is simple: You must receive His gifts by faith. If your mind thinks and believes that God is causing or allowing your problems, you are not looking for or anticipating His goodness to pour into your life. If this is the way you've been seeing God, you have work to do to renew your mind and conform your thoughts with the truth.

As you begin believing for and expecting "good and perfect gifts" to come into your life, you put yourself in position to receive from the "Father of lights" instead of receiving from the father of darkness — the devil.

God Never Changes, and the Quality of His Gifts Never Changes

James then adds that with God, the Father of lights, there is "no variableness, neither shadow of turning." These words in Greek specifically describe *the shifting shadows of a Roman sundial*. A sundial tells the time of day as time passes and the sun moves across the sky. As the sun moves, the shadow on the sundial shifts to reflect the accurate time. This means every time you look at a sundial, the shadow has changed and is changing; it is technically never the same.

By using the words "the Father of lights, with whom is no variableness, neither shadow of turning," James was saying, "God is not like a Roman sundial with regards to what He gives you. There is no variableness or changing in what He provides. What comes from Him is always a steady flow of *good and perfect gifts*." That means when tragedy comes, you don't need to stop and wonder if it is from God or the enemy.

Anything that enters your life to bring damage, destruction, or ruin it is *not* from God. But if what comes to you is good, beneficial, completing, and perfecting, it *is* from God. On this issue of what God gives and what He *never* gives, there is no variableness or shadow of turning. He never changes.

STUDY QUESTIONS

Study to shew thyself approved unto God, a workman that needeth not to be ashamed, rightly dividing the word of truth.
— 2 Timothy 2:15

Stop and ask yourself: *How do I see God?* If you have an inaccurate view of who He is, you need to humble yourself before Him and allow His Spirit to renew your mind. Carefully read Romans 12:2; Ephesians 4:22-24; James 1:21-25; Psalm 1:1-3; and Joshua 1:8. According to these passages:

1. What does renewing your mind on a daily basis look like?
2. What positive results can you expect?
3. How is what you're learning from God's Word in these lessons renewing your mind with a more accurate view of God's character?

PRACTICAL APPLICATION

> **But be ye doers of the word, and not hearers only, deceiving your own selves.**
> **—James 1:22**

1. Are you presently in a deep, dark place of hardship or suffering? If so, briefly describe what you are experiencing and what has helped you to keep trusting God in the midst of it.
2. The Christians that James wrote to believed that God, from a distance, was allowing the tragic events to come into their lives for some strange reason. Be honest: Is this what you have believed as you have walked through dark, difficult times?
3. Are there any specific ways of thinking or speaking about God that you sense He wants you to change?

LESSON 4

TOPIC
If You Need Wisdom

SCRIPTURES

4. **James 1:1-3** — James, a servant of God and of the Lord Jesus Christ, to the twelve tribes which are scattered abroad, greeting. My brethren, count it all joy when ye fall into divers temptations. Knowing this, that the trying of your faith worketh patience.
5. **James 1:13** — Let no man say when he is tempted, I am tempted of God: for God cannot be tempted with evil, neither tempteth he any man

6. **James 1:17** — Every good gift and every perfect gift is from above, and cometh down from the Father of lights, with whom is no variableness, neither shadow of turning.

GREEK WORDS

1. "scattered abroad" — **διασπορά** (*diaspora*): the random scattering of seed; used to depict the scattering of Jewish believers
2. "tempted" — **πειράζω** (*peiradzo*): to test, try, or tempt; to cause one to fail, to falter, to stumble, or to bring destruction; depicts a calculated test to bring about failure; used to denote the actions of the devil, the tempter, or of the Pharisees and Sadducees
3. "of" — **ἀπὸ** (*apo*): away from; denotes something done from a distance or something that is done remotely
4. "evil" — **κακός** (*kakos*): evil, vile, foul, or destructive
5. "good" — **ἀγαθός** (*agathos*): anything good, beneficial, or profitable
6. "gift" — **δόσις** (*dosis*): perpetual giving from God; the habitual giving of God
7. "perfect" — **τέλειον** (*teleion*): mature, complete, or perfect
8. "cometh down" — **καταβαίνω** (*katabaino*): to be dominated or subjugated by something coming down very hard, like a downpour of rain
9. "there is no variableness, neither shadow of turning" — describes, for example, the shifting shadows of a Roman sundial
10. "brethren" — **ἀδελφός** (*adelphos*): a term used to describe two or more who were born from the same womb; later used in a military sense to depict brothers in battle; a comrade
11. "count it" — **ἡγέομαι** (*hegeomai*): to reckon; to determine; pictures a determination not left to chance
12. "joy" — **χαρά** (*chara*): joy, not happiness
13. "ye fall" — **περιπίπτω** (*peripipto*): pictures falling into a deep ditch; in context, to be completely surrounded by encompassing problems
14. "trying" — **δοκιμάζω** (*dokimadzo*): pictures the process of testing a product to see if it can live up to its reputation; to determine the quality of a thing; to determine if a product or claim is as good as it is asserted to be; to authenticate; to prove

SYNOPSIS

Thousands of Christians were taken as prisoners and forced to chisel out the Titus Tunnel near the ancient Port of Salacia. Because of their faith in Christ, they found themselves trapped in a deep, dark place with no apparent way of escape.

Interestingly, there is an ancient staircase in the tunnel that leads to the top and outside, but it doesn't connect with the tunnel's floor. Visually, it appears like an unattainable leap to get from the floor to the staircase, yet it is possible to reach it if one is told how.

Are you in a similar situation? Can you see the "staircase" that leads out of your mess, but you don't know the specific steps needed to reach those stairs? Here's good news! If you need wisdom, God has it in abundance. And He is willing to give you all the answers you need to get out of the trap you're in — if you will seek His presence and obey what He tells you to do.

The emphasis of this lesson:
Deciding to stay in joy regardless of what's going on around you is the first step to getting out of any trap set by the enemy. Joy is a work of God's grace deep inside of you. It is a supernatural strength that will carry you out of the deepest ditch and into God's destiny for your life.

To Whom Was James Writing?

James, the half-brother of Jesus and bishop of the church in Jerusalem, opened his letter saying, "James, a servant of God and of the Lord Jesus Christ, to the twelve tribes which are scattered abroad…" (James 1:1). Although these words were inspired by the Spirit of God for all believers *for all generations*, the people James was writing to were believers who had been "scattered abroad."

We've seen in the previous lessons that the words "scattered abroad" are from the Greek word *diaspora*, and it describes *the random scattering of seed*. The Holy Spirit used this Greek word to explain what had happened to James' readers. They had been ripped from their homeland and their businesses — separated from their families and friends — and randomly scattered like seeds all across the eastern Roman Empire. In the process, they had lost everything. Now they were writing to James, looking and longing for answers as to what God was doing in the midst of all they were experiencing.

James Strongly Rebuked His Readers

Weary from the persecution they had endured, these scattered believers began to question God's level of involvement in their hardships. This is revealed in James 1:13 when James repeats the very words they had been saying: "Let no man say when he is tempted, I am tempted of God: for God cannot be tempted with evil, neither tempteth he any man."

We have discovered that the phrase "Let no man say" in the Greek is a strong prohibition or rebuke. It literally means, "I hear what you're saying, and it's not right. So stop it and stop it now. Don't talk like that anymore." What were they saying that James was so adamant about? When they were being tempted, they were saying, "I am being tempted of God."

The word "tempted" here is the Greek word *peiradzo*, and it describes *a calculated test designed to bring a person down*. It is *a test designed to cause one to fail, to falter, to stumble*, or *to bring destruction*. It describes the act of *destruction, decimation*, or *being crushed*. This verse could actually be translated, "Let no man say when his life is being crushed and destroyed, 'I'm being crushed and destroyed of God.'"

We have seen that that word "of" in Greek is the word *apo*, which means *away from*. It denotes *something done from a distance*. The use of *apo* here implies that these Christians believed God was doing something remotely. They were beginning to believe that although He didn't personally, directly bring destruction into their lives, He did it *from a distance*. "God is God," they were saying. "And if He had wanted to stop these hardships, He could have stopped them. Therefore, since He didn't stop these things, it must somehow be His will for us to go through them."

This type of thinking was wrong, and that is why James essentially told them, "Let no man say when he is tempted that God is causing it. How *dare* you say this! How can you even *think* that God would do such things to you? That is just not the nature of God."

Then James Gave Them a Picture of God's True Nature

James revealed the true nature of God by describing what He always gives. He said, "Every good gift and every perfect gift is from above, and cometh down from the Father of lights, with whom is no variableness, neither shadow of turning" (James 1:17).

We saw in the previous lesson that the word "good" is the Greek word *agathos*, and it describes *anything good, beneficial, or profitable*. The word "gift" in Greek is the word *dosis*, and it conveys *the perpetual, habitual giving action of God*. Giving "good gifts" is not what He does occasionally; it's what He does *always*. Everything that comes from God is good, and it is always beneficial.

James goes on to say that not only are God's gifts good, but they are also "perfect." The word "perfect" is from the word *telion*, which describes *something that completes, matures, or adds to your life*. Thus, when we receive something from God in Heaven, it never *takes away* — it always *adds to*. What God gives perfects and completes us.

That's how you can discern whether something is from God or not. If what comes into your life takes from you, it is not from God.

To really hammer home this issue of what God gives and what He never gives, James said that with God, there is "no variableness, neither shadow of turning." This phrase in the Greek actually describes *the shifting shadows of a Roman sundial*. As the earth rotates on its axis and time passes, the shadow of the sun on the sundial continually changes to mark the time of day.

James incorporates this illustration to tell us that when it comes to the issue of giving "good and perfect gifts," God is *nothing like* the Roman sundial. He *never* changes. Unlike the shadow on the sundial that is constantly shifting, God stays the same. Therefore, you can always expect good and perfect things from Him.

As Believers, We Are 'Brethren'

To encourage his readers — both then and now — James said, "My brethren, count it all joy when ye fall into divers temptations" (James 1:2). Notice the use of the word "brethren." This is from the Greek word *adelphos*, a term used to describe *two or more who were born from the same womb*. It was later used in a military sense to depict *brothers in battle; comrades*.

Interestingly, the word *adelphos* was first made popular by Alexander the Great, notably one of the greatest soldiers in human history. From time to time, he would wrap his arm around another soldier who had been especially brave and call him *adelphos*. It was his way of saying, "Brother, you and I are in this fight together."

The word *adelphos* carried the idea of *camaraderie*. By using this word, James was telling his readers that he was proud of them. He didn't condemn them for struggling in their faith or for having a wrong understanding of God's role regarding temptation. He was proud of them for still being in the fight. In the same way, we need to reach out to our "fellow soldiers" and encourage them for not giving up despite the difficulties they are facing.

Make a Decision To Be in Joy

Next, James said, "…Count it all joy when ye fall into divers temptations." The phrase "count it" is from the Greek word *hegeomai*, which means *to reckon; to determine*. It pictures *a determination not left to chance*. When James said, "Count it all joy," he was saying, "Determine joy — make a decision to be in joy. Don't leave it to doubt, feelings, or chance."

The word *hegeomai* is also used in Romans 6:11 where the apostle Paul said, "Likewise reckon ye also yourselves to be dead indeed unto sin, but alive unto God through Jesus Christ our Lord." The word "reckon" is the Greek word *hegeomai*. This means that when sin tries to show up in your life, rather than tolerate it or just hope it goes away, you need to *reckon* it dead. That is, make a decision and determine it dead. Don't waver or leave it to chance. At the same time, *reckon* yourself alive unto God. In other words, *make a decision to allow the Spirit of Christ to fully operate inside of you*.

In both verses, *hegeomai* depicts a predetermined course of action. Essentially, James told his readers, "You need to make a decision that you're going to have joy in your life regardless of what you're experiencing. It is not just going to happen automatically. You need to *decide* on it."

Go for Joy, Not Happiness

Happiness and joy are not the same. James didn't say, "Try to be *happy* when you fall into divers temptations." He said, "Count it all *joy*." The word "joy" is the Greek word *chara*, and *chara* is a derivative of the word *charis*, which is the Greek word for *grace*. Therefore, when the Bible talks about joy, it is talking about a quality produced deep inside of us by the grace of God.

Happiness is like the ripples on the surface of a lake or river. The top of the water is affected by the environment and atmospheric conditions, and it is changing all the time. One day it's smooth, and the next day it's rough. But deep down near the bottom of that lake or river, the water conditions stay virtually unchanged. Regardless of what's happening on the surface, the inside remains steady and consistent. That is what joy is like — it is unchanging.

God doesn't want us to live like the water on the surface, constantly moved by what is happening in our environment: When circumstances are good, we're happy, but when they're bad, we're not happy. Instead, He wants us to live deeper — He wants us to go for *joy*. Happiness is fleeting; it comes and it goes. But joy is a work of grace produced by the Holy Spirit deep inside us. It remains the same regardless of what is happening on the exterior of our lives.

Choosing joy is the first step to getting out of any trap the enemy has set. This attitudinal change is a daily, sometimes moment-by-moment, decision. It is an inner determination that says, *I'm no longer going to be swayed by circumstances, nor am I going to follow the ups and downs of my emotions. I'm going to jump into the current of joy deep inside me. It is going to carry me out of this dark place to where God wants me to be.*

'Count It All Joy' *When* You Fall Into Major Hardships

Like James' readers, you are to "count it all joy when ye fall into divers temptations" (James 1:2). The words "ye fall" is the Greek word *peripipto*, and it pictures *one falling into a deep ditch headfirst*. In context, it means *to be completely surrounded by encompassing problems*.

The word *peripipto* is only used one other place in Scripture — in Luke 10:30 in the story of the Good Samaritan. A man who was traveling to Jericho "fell among thieves, which stripped him of his raiment, and wounded him, and departed, leaving him half dead." The phrase "fell among" is the same Greek word *peripipto*. This innocent man was surrounded on all sides by thieves, and they stripped him, robbed him, wounded him, and left him for dead.

When James talks about the divers temptations "you fall" into, he is talking about major hardships that *strip you down, rob you blind, wound you deeply*, and *leave you at death's door*. When you fall into these kinds of disastrous events, make a decision to jump into that deeper flow of joy. Choose not to be affected by the circumstances on the surface. The attitude of joy will take you into the victory that Jesus has planned for your life.

Interestingly, even the word "when" in James 1:2 has significance. Its tense here describes *something that will take you off-guard and by surprise*, which is exactly the way the devil attacks. The truth is, no matter how long we have walked with God or how spiritual we are, all of us experience a "when" moment of attack when the enemy throws a calculated test our way that takes us completely by surprise. The Holy Spirit knows it's coming, so He mercifully tells us what to do in this verse so we'll be ready for it.

Always Keep in Mind What the Testing Is Producing

James describes the temptations we face using the word "divers." Interestingly, it is the same word used in Genesis 37 to describe Joseph's coat of "many" colors. Thus, when James says, "…Count it all joy when ye fall into *divers* temptations," he is letting us know that the devil's temptations are *multicolored*. That is, they come in all shapes and sizes, so don't think they are always going to be the same. Nevertheless, whatever he sends our way, we have the God-given ability to overcome it.

Something else to keep in mind is what James tells in verse 3 of chapter 1: "Knowing this, that the trying of your faith worketh patience." The phrase "knowing this" is ongoing in the Greek tense, which means you would translate it as, "Knowing and knowing and knowing." It indicates *never forgetting; always knowing; and keeping it at the front of your mind*. It's almost as if James is reaching through the pages of Scripture to grab hold of us to shake us and say, "Know this! Know this! Know this! Always keep this in your mind: The trying of your faith worketh patience."

The word "trying" in this verse is the Greek word *dokimadzo*, and it pictures *the process of testing a product to see if it can live up to its reputation*.

It is *a test to determine the quality of a thing — to determine if a product or claim is as good as it is asserted to be.* It also means *to authenticate or to prove.*

For example, if someone had a product and advertised boastfully about how great it was, someone might come along and say, "I heard your advertisement. Now I'm going to test your product to see if it is really as good as you're claiming it is." That person would then begin to vigorously test it to see if it was everything it was advertised to be. That's what the word "trying" means. It describes *the process of authentication.*

James was telling his reader *and us,* "When the devil comes to test you, he is coming to test your statement of faith. Your words were an advertisement to the spirit realm, and the devil heard it. Now he's coming to test (*dokimadzo*) you out to see if you (the product) are as good as you claim." Are you really committed to your confession of faith? Are you committed to your healing, your marriage, your finances, and your church? Are you as committed as your boast is? Each test he brings is your opportunity to authenticate and prove that your faith is real. It is also a chance for patience to be developed, which is what we will focus on in our next lesson.

STUDY QUESTIONS
**Study to shew thyself approved unto God, a workman that needeth not to be ashamed, rightly dividing the word of truth.
— 2 Timothy 2:15**

1. How is the Roman sundial alluded to in James 1:17 and the principle of Hebrews 13:8 connected? (Also consider Numbers 23:19, First Samuel 15:29, and Malachi 3:6.)
2. To help you choose joy, there are specific actions you can take. According to Philippians 4:8 and Psalm 77:11 and 12, what can you do to stir up joy and gratefulness within you?
3. Do you need more of God's *grace* to stay in joy? Read James 4:6 and First Peter 5:5. What do these promises say to you? What do you need to do to receive more grace from God? (Also consider Psalm 84:11 and Second Corinthians 9:8.)

PRACTICAL APPLICATION

> **But be ye doers of the word, and not hearers only, deceiving your own selves.**
> **—James 1:22**

1. In your own words, briefly explain the unchanging nature of God revealed in James 1:17. What does He *always* do, and what does He *never* do? Why do you think it is vital to understand this?
2. Who has been a great source of encouragement to you in your Christian walk? Why not take a few moments to say *thank you* through a text, an email, a card, a call, or a gift?
3. Do you know of fellow "brethren" who could use encouragement? Who can you reach your arm around and encourage as your "brethren" (*adelphos*) just as others have encouraged you?

LESSON 5

TOPIC

The Right Way To Ask in Faith

SCRIPTURES

1. James 1:2-8 — My brethren, count it all joy when ye fall into divers temptations; knowing this, that the trying of your faith worketh patience. But let patience have her perfect work, that ye may be perfect and entire, wanting nothing. If any of you lack wisdom, let him ask of God, that giveth to all men liberally, and upbraideth not; and it shall be given him. But let him ask in faith, nothing wavering. For he that wavereth is like a wave of the sea driven with the wind and tossed. For let not that man think that he shall receive any thing of the Lord. A double minded man is unstable in all his ways.

GREEK WORDS

1. "brethren" — ἀδελφός (*adelphos*): a term used to describe two or more who were born from the same womb; later used in a military sense to depict brothers in battle; a comrade

2. "count it" — ἡγέομαι (*hegeomai*): to reckon; to determine; pictures a determination not left to chance
3. "joy" — χαρά (*chara*): joy, not happiness
4. "ye fall" — περιπίπτω (*peripipto*): pictures falling into a deep ditch; in context, to be completely surrounded by encompassing problems
5. "trying" — δοκιμάζω (*dokimadzo*): pictures the process of testing a product to see if it can live up to its reputation; to determine the quality of a thing; to determine if a product or claim is as good as it is asserted to be; to authenticate; to prove
6. "worketh" — κατεργάζομαι (*katergadzomai*): to work down from the top to the bottom; to thoroughly work throughout
7. "patience" — ὑπομονή (*hupomone*): pictures defiantly sticking it out regardless of pressures mounted against it; staying power; "hang-in-there" power; the attitude that holds out, holds on, outlasts, perseveres, and hangs in there, never giving up, refusing to surrender to obstacles, and turning down every opportunity to quit; pictures one who is under a heavy load, but refuses to bend, break, or surrender
8. "perfect" — τέλειον (*teleion*): mature leaving behind; pictures a deficiency of any type
9. "entire" — ὁλόκληρος (*holokleros*): depicts possessing everything allotted to one by inheritance
10. "wanting" (v. 4), "lack" (v. 5) — λείπω (*leipo*): leaving behind; pictures a deficiency of any type
11. "wisdom" — σοφός (*sophos*): pictures wisdom not naturally attained; specially insightful
12. "ask" — αἰτέω (*aiteo*): to request, beseech, petition, or demand; to ask with full expectation of receiving what was firmly requested
13. "of" — παρά (*para*): alongside
14. "liberally" — ἁπλῶς (*haplos*): pictures something given generously, abundantly, plentifully, profusely, bountifully, and open-handedly; copiously, amply, extravagantly, lavishly, liberally, plentifully, or richly; can also mean directly, simply, or sincerely
15. "upbraideth" — ὀνειδίζω (*oneididzo*): to nitpick
16. "doubleminded" — δίψυχος (*dipsuchos*): two-souled; double-minded; pictures one who vacillates back and forth constantly, complete, or perfect

SYNOPSIS

In an effort to redirect the excess rainwater coming down from the mountains and stop the flooding that was occurring near the ancient Port of Salacia, the Titus Tunnel was constructed. Using hammers and chisels, this passageway was carved out of sold rock by Jews and Christians who were sent to the site as slaves and prisoners. The working conditions were deplorable, and the provision of bread and water alone was not enough to sustain the workers through the physical demands of the project. For many believers, the Titus Tunnel was a trap from which they wondered if they would ever escape.

Maybe you're wondering the same thing about the difficulties you're facing. The good news is, no matter how deep or dark your situation, it is not your destiny. God has a plan to put you in a better place, and developing an attitude of faith is a major key to your doorway out.

The emphasis of this lesson:

The trying of your faith infuses you with the supernatural empowerment called patience. As this divine endurance works within you, it brings you into greater levels of spiritual maturity, positioning you to possess the fullness of your inheritance in Christ.

Joy Will Carry You Through

"My brethren, count it all joy when ye fall into divers temptations" (James 1:2). These were the first words uttered by James to the suffering believers who had been scattered abroad across the Roman Empire. It is the same words the Holy Spirit is still speaking to us today as we encounter times of testing. In our last lesson, we learned that the phrase "count it" is the Greek word *hegeomai*, which means *to determine* or *to reckon*. By using this word, James was saying, "When you fall into temptations, make a solid decision that you are going to have joy."

"Joy" is the Greek word *chara*, which is a form of *charis*, the Greek word for *grace*. Joy is not happiness. Happiness is fleeting. Like the ripples that come and go on the top of a lake or river, our level of happiness vacillates greatly. Joy, on the other hand, is like the strong current that consistently flows along the bottom of a river. It is a divine force produced by the grace of God that carries us through every situation, right into victory.

When are we to "count it all joy"? James said when "ye fall into temptations." The phrase "ye fall" is the Greek word *peripipto*, which pictures *one falling into a deep ditch or being completely surrounded by encompassing problems*. Every time we find ourselves surrounded on every side by trouble, we are to make a choice to stay in joy. As we line up our thinking and speaking with truth, we will have what we need to make it out of any mess the devil has made for us.

The Enemy Will 'Try' Your Faith

James continued in verse 3 saying, "Knowing this, that the trying of your faith worketh patience." The words "knowing this" are ongoing in Greek, which means it would be better translated as *knowing, knowing, knowing....* It is a continuous, uninterrupted action. In other words, James was saying, "This is something you are to always know, never forget, and keep at the forefront of your mind." What are you to always be mindful of and never forget? "That the trying of your faith worketh patience."

The word "trying" here is the Greek word *dokimadzo*, and its meaning is very different than the word "tempted" (*peiradzo*) in James 1:13. The word *dokimadzo* pictures *the process of testing a product to see if it can live up to its reputation*. It is *a test to determine the quality of a thing or to determine if a product or claim is as good as it is asserted to be*. It is a test *to authenticate* or *to prove*.

If you have been declaring by faith that you're going to walk in divine health or be financially blessed or be more loving and kind toward others, the enemy has heard you. He and his cohorts are going to put your claims to the test to see if you are going to live up to what you have boasted. So don't be surprised if he attempts to strike you with sickness, drain your finances, or send a stream of obnoxious people your way. He is bent on "trying" (*dokimadzo*) your faith.

Your confession of faith will almost always trigger a negative response from Satan. But don't lose heart or give up. See every form of opposition as an opportunity to prove and authenticate your faith. When you chose to push back against the enemy, something supernatural begins to happen — it "worketh patience."

Pushing Back Against His Attacks Produces Empowerment

The word "worketh" is the Greek word *katergadzomai*, which is the compound of two words: the word *kata*, which describes *something that comes down or dominates*, and the word *ergadzomai*, which means *work* or *energy*. When these two words are combined to form *katergadzomai*, it describes *something that starts at the top and works down to the bottom, thoroughly working throughout your entire being*.

This word "worketh" describes a person who has been supernaturally energized. When you choose to push back against the enemy's attack, a divine empowerment takes place, which begins at the top of your head and works its way down to your feet. The Bible calls this empowerment "patience."

The word "patience" is the Greek word *hupomone*, which is the compound of two words: *hupo*, which means *to be under*, and the word *meno*, which means *to abide or stay*. When these two words are combined to form *hupomone*, it pictures *a person defiantly sticking it out regardless of pressures mounted against it*. The word *hupomone* also means *staying power, "hang-in-there" power, the attitude that holds out, holds on, outlasts, perseveres, and hangs in there, never giving up, refusing to surrender to obstacles, and turning down every opportunity to quit*. It depicts *one who is under a heavy load, but refuses to bend, break, or surrender*.

When you sum it all up, "patience" — the Greek word *hupomone* — is really *endurance*. Every time you chose to stand and fight against the enemy's attacks — trusting and speaking God's Word instead of focusing on what is overwhelming you or on what you see or feel — you are energized by divine patience. This process of empowerment is what we need to *know that we know that we know*: The trying of our faith worketh "patience" (James 1:3).

Do You Want To Receive Your Full Inheritance?

Then James said, "But let patience have her perfect work, that ye may be perfect and entire, wanting nothing" (James 1:4). The word "perfect" describes *something that is complete*. It is a derivative of the Greek word *telos*, which means that patience will bring you into *a stage of spiritual maturity*. It will also make you "entire," which is the Greek word *holokleros*, and it depicts *a family or an individual who possesses everything originally allotted by inheritance.* The word *holokleros* is a picture of one who hasn't lost anything that has been given to him. That person is standing in his full inheritance.

Through Jesus Christ, you have a rich inheritance. It includes healing, deliverance, prosperity, peace, joy, healthy relationships, and countless other blessings. To receive and stand in your full inheritance, you have to allow God's divine patience (endurance) to continue its work in you. As you do, the Bible says you will be "perfect and entire, wanting nothing."

The word "wanting" is a derivative of the Greek word *leipo*, which describes *a deficiency of any kind.* Thus, as you make a decision to jump into joy and stay in faith — trusting and standing on God's Word and allowing patience to work in you — in the end, you will not be deficient in any way.

You Have Questions — God Has Answers

Now you may be thinking, *I've done all this. I've tried my best to trust God's Word and walk by faith, not by what I see. I've been patient and have endured through many difficulties. But I'm still being slammed by one problem after another. Why is this not working for me in my life?*

Your answer can be found in James 1:5.

James 1:5 says, "If any of you lack wisdom, let him ask of God, that giveth to all men liberally, and upbraideth not; and it shall be given him." When you have a question, God has an answer ready to deliver to you! No one can see your situation and what's going on inside you like God can. He has x-ray eyes and is able to pinpoint the problem and give you precise solutions to overcome it.

The word "lack" in verse 5 is again a derivative of the Greek word *leipo*, which describes *a deficiency of any kind.* If you are deficient in wisdom in any way, God invites you to ask Him for answers. The word "wisdom" here is the Greek word *sophos*, which describes *special insight.* Hence, if you need *special insight* into your struggle — *special insight* as to why your faith doesn't seem to be working — James says you are to ask of God.

The word "ask" is the Greek word *aiteo*, which means *to request, beseech, petition,* or *demand.* It means *to ask with full expectation of receiving what was firmly requested.* A good example of the use of this word is when Joseph of Arimathea came to Pilate and asked for Jesus' body after He had been crucified. Mark 15:43 says he "…went boldly unto Pilate, and craved the body of Jesus." The word "craved" is the Greek word *aiteo* — the same word translated as "ask" in James 1:5. Joseph demanded the body of Jesus and fully expected to receive what he asked for. This is what God encourages you to do when you need wisdom, or special insight. You are to "ask of Him."

Interestingly, even the word "of" is significant here. It is the Greek word *para*, which means *alongside*. God's one stipulation to receiving wisdom regarding your situation is that you come *alongside* (*para*) Him. He wants you to get as close to Him as you can, and then He will open His hand and show you everything you need to know.

Our God is the God of the open hand, not the clenched fist. And when you choose to *para* Him (come *alongside* Him), all that He is begins to be released into your life. The Greek rendering of James 1:5 actually says, "If any of you lack wisdom, let him ask of the *Giving God*...." The truth is, He will not withhold one good thing from you as you abide in fellowship with Him. That is what He craves from you — a genuine relationship. You don't have to beg Him; you just need to *abide in Him*.

The Bible says He "...giveth to all men liberally, and upbraideth not...." The word "upbraideth" in the Greek means *to nitpick*. God is not a nit-picker. That is, He's not waiting for you to come to Him so He can point out all your faults and weaknesses. He loves you and wants to help you. His arms are open wide and He is ready to "liberally" give you the wisdom you need. That word "liberally" is the Greek word *haplos*, and it pictures *something given generously, abundantly, plentifully, profusely, bountifully, and open-handedly*. God is excited to answer your questions; if you will just come *alongside* Him, He will open His hand and extravagantly bless you.

Simply Ask in Faith Without Wavering

James rounds out his divine instructions, saying, "But let him ask in faith, nothing wavering. For he that wavereth is like a wave of the sea driven with the wind and tossed. For let not that man think that he shall receive any thing of the Lord. A double minded man is unstable in all his ways" (James 1:6-8).

Once you are close to God, you must ask Him for wisdom in faith without wavering. The Bible says those that waver or doubt are "double minded," which is the Greek word *dipsuchos*, and it means *two-souled*. It pictures *one who vacillates back and forth constantly*. It would be like a one person having two heads: One head would desire and say one thing, and the other head would desire and say another thing. There would be constant conflict and arguing, and the person would essentially go nowhere. Like a wave on the sea, they would simply rock back and forth.

James uses the word *dipsuchos* to paint a picture of what some people look like when they pray — like a man with two heads, speaking two different things. God said, "For let not that man think that he shall receive any thing of the Lord" (James 1:7). God wants to bless us, but trying to bless someone who is double-minded is like trying to hit a moving target.

So make your decision to lock your faith into God's Word, and don't budge. When you ask in faith without wavering, your faith becomes a stationary target God can easily hit. This is where the blessing of patience comes into play. As you allow the Holy Spirit to work in you the supernatural "hang in there" power of patience, or endurance, He will enable you to stand firm on His promises and receive exactly what you ask for as you come alongside and abide in your relationship with Him.

STUDY QUESTIONS

Study to shew thyself approved unto God, a workman that needeth not to be ashamed, rightly dividing the word of truth.
— 2 Timothy 2:15

1. What declarations of faith have you recently made? Which specific scriptures are you standing on and speaking?
2. Has the enemy come against you in these areas? If so, how?
3. In order to receive God's wisdom (*special insight*), He requires you to draw close to Him. According to Scripture, what happens when you draw close to God? What can you expect from spending time in His presence? (Consider James 4:8; Psalm 16:11; 145:18, 19; John 15:4-7; and Isaiah 40:29-31.)

PRACTICAL APPLICATION

But be ye doers of the word, and not hearers only, deceiving your own selves.
— James 1:22

1. Be honest. How did you view patience *before* going through this lesson? How has your perspective of patience changed?
2. Are you looking and longing for answers to certain situations you're facing? With what specific issues do you need special insight? Take time now to get alone with the Lord and pray. Ask Him to speak words of direction to you concerning each of these things.

A Prayer To Receive Salvation

If you've never received Jesus as your Savior and Lord, now is the time for you to experience the new life Jesus wants to give you! To receive God's gift of salvation that can be obtained through Jesus alone, pray this prayer from your heart:

> *Jesus, I repent of my sin and receive You as my Savior and Lord. Wash away my sin with Your precious blood and make me completely new. I thank You that my sin is removed, and Satan no longer has any right to lay claim on me. Through Your empowering grace, I faithfully promise that I will serve You as my Lord for the rest of my life.*

If you just prayed this prayer of salvation, you are born again! You are a brand-new creation in Christ! Would you please let us know of your decision by going to **renner.org/salvation**? We would love to connect with you and pray for you as you begin your new life in Christ.

Scriptures for further study: John 3:16; John 14:6; Acts 4:12; Ephesians 1:7; Hebrews 10:19,20; 1 Peter 1:18,19; Romans 10:9,10; Colossians 1:13; 2 Corinthians 5:17; Romans 6:4; 1 Peter 1:3

Notes

Notes

CLAIM YOUR FREE RESOURCE!

As a way of introducing you further to the teaching ministry of Rick Renner, we would like to send you FREE of charge his teaching, "How To Receive a Miraculous Touch From God" on CD or as an MP3 download.

In His earthly ministry, Jesus commonly healed *all* who were sick of *all* their diseases. In this profound message, learn about the manifold dimensions of Christ's wisdom, goodness, power, and love toward all humanity who came to Him in faith with their needs.

☑ **YES, I want to receive Rick Renner's monthly teaching letter!**

Simply scan the QR code to claim this resource or go to:
renner.org/claim-your-free-offer

WITH US!

 renner.org

- facebook.com/rickrenner • facebook.com/rennerdenise
- youtube.com/rennerministries • youtube.com/deniserenner
- instagram.com/rickrrenner • instagram.com/rennerministries_ instagram.com/rennerdenise

www.ingramcontent.com/pod-product-compliance
Lightning Source LLC
Chambersburg PA
CBHW071650040426
42452CB00009B/1821